Broken Prose, Spoken Poems

Free verse by
Clifford Schrage

**For my writing students
who've come to love
the finest words
set in their finest order.**

Copyright 2016 by the author

ISBN 978-1-987852-06-6

Published by Wood Islands Prints; 670 TCH RR1; Belle River, PE C0A 1B0; Canada

The author can be reached via email at
sherryandcliff@gmail.com
Copies of this book can be purchased from the author and are also available at amazon.com

Cliff Schrage is a high school creative writing, film studies, and literature teacher. He is a father of eight (six adopted) and grandfather of four. His novels include A Fruitful Field *and* Silas Dillon Of Cary County, *and his poetry has appeared in various periodicals in North America. He makes his home on Long Island, New York; and in the summer he resides on Prince Edward Island, Canada.*

COYOTES

We never see you, you elusive canine knaves,
diminutive wolves,
coy cousins of conquered pets,
committers of murders,
moon shadow chasers,
gang members hiding from light taking
night's quiet by her throat in long crescendos of cries,
pup yips, whelp barks, snarls,
howling wails pitched high as whistles—
social celebrations over bloody kills.

We never see, but ever hear
these suffused pitches, your singing of
"a land of darkness and the shadow of death."
At the food chain summit and summer's quiet gloom
you howl wails pitched high as whistles
heard in the nether east of Eden,
stealing serenity, taking her by the throat in
this fallen world. Your frenzy of a dozen dialoguing voices
startles the stillness in stars at the treetops of the universe,
stills faint pulses of contiguous creatures
in your bloody desperation, your
desperate despair—
like humans in their social loneliness
in this fallen world.

SWANS

As sallow, ashen angels
these lean fowl fly
beneath clear heavens
in the lavender evening.

Saintly over a smooth waveless surface
as ancient ships in white canvas,
silent on an indolent inlet
they drift, sail.

Nothing flutters
or shifts
in moments of moving time
until the swans'

Wings widen,
slam air under necks stretched forward;
webbed feet slap across a surface of water
in the lumbering dusk.

This sound swallows silence
in sudden turbulence;
the swans launch, softening their noise,
lifting upward, rising toward heaven

in vast white flight.
All earth's fixed
this moment—with this flock's motion
and is still.

ACROSS THE RUBBLE OF BABEL

They see us across the water—

Publics of another culture.

Uniting is strained.
For centuries a band of water separates us.

They see us beneath evening darkness,
Across the rubble of Babel

And water.
Lights flickering—

We see them—
Flickering lights.

Our hands, feet, the way we eat, fight, live—
Like them for centuries.

Two sides. Us and them,
We and they, couplets—

They see us. We see them—
Lights flicker

SHARON, VERMONT

This is the other side of the world
Where dairy cows remain docile,
Dressed in panda bear clothes, bashful—
Grazing in daisy-dappled, green walls of pastures,
Ascending.

Dusk descends on talons,
And clouds are mountains in white and gray, or
Cumulus peaches enthroned over walls of emerald green.
White River is yellow-silver while this slow dusk
Descends.

We begin to drop into sleep, drowsing into
That place where time is sly—
The sound of still crickets slow dancing
With humming chime of moving water,
Both alone.

When dawn rises,
One red barn yawns,
Demanding all the attention.
On the other side of the world
Dusk descends.

NOVEMBER

In the Michigan village
By the lake at the base of the hill
Fat turkeys wrestle fat hands,
Stern human eyes.

Stout axe to oak stump, cold steel to soft throats—
Folks watch and mock;
Birds run amuck in blood,
Drop dead, headless.

Under enormous barren elms
Old folks stroll streets. others indoors peer out windows.
In the market the butcher weighs the farmer's work
On a balance scale.

Crimson, gold, and yellow leaves
Have fallen to huddle to curbs and fences,
Fallen into brown,
To wither to mulch.

HERMITS

Hermits live in these hills,
Nomads on these roads.
Who will go? Who will reach them?
We saw the far forsythias splattering yellow paint,
And the white poplars popping open on the perimeters of fields
Early in silver spring.

We're fat,
Prone on a raft in a pool, cool,
Hands clasped behind head,
Cigar in jaw,
Eyes closed,
Facing heaven, sleeping.

Harvest fields burst with whiteness,
Chasing, calling laborers.
Who will come before winter?
Hermits live in these hills,
Nomads on these roads.
Who will go? Who will reach them?

LONG ROAD

The road creeps slowly on its belly
Portland to Fort Lauderdale,
Tail to tongue.

We hear the ocean's baritone voice in broken cadence
Murmuring songs through hours of soaring owls,
See its slow dance with the moon.

We enfold the coast in the cushioned world of this car
Passing acres and acres of sea,
Wishing...wishing... with the ocean, praying.

AUTUMN SWAMP MAPLE

Look far down Brown's River, see
The swamp maple—all orange
Among tupelos and cattails.

Once you trudged through thorns and marsh,
Found this tree,
Climbed its branches.

Each leaf held many colors—
Rose, sunflower, and sunrise
Over summer green.

NEW YEAR'S DAY

In the frozen pile of the snow plow's push
Chunks of curbside ice sit
Like stones in
Russet speckles in white sand.
Someone shuffles warily to the corner.
A whole year has fallen like a parcel
Into the mailbox
huddled in South Dakota coldness—
Empty, alone, blue.

AFTER A STORM

Around root clusters of trees,
Sunken logs,
Rusted shopping carts,
Cinder blocks, bald tires, junk men have dumped;
Sticks and leaves float swiftly eastward
Toward the tide of Forge River.

Here behind the market you bend over the soft moss of this stream bank.
After the storm sunlight breaks, water still falling from bare Limbs
Above you.

Small plants under currents bend gilded green.
Sand ripples, loosening minute roots.
Tiny westbound minnows suspending in emerald midwater,
Are forced backward, then jolted forward, inches farther west.
In pure unsullied strength—
With no show of strain—
As though their tiny minds had will,
These slight fish find their way beside the bank
In a cove with little current
For rest.

Here you hear a shuttering song of one bird stirring
    solitary.
Here you hear the market's racket afar, the roar of the
    highway farther,
This tranquil water moving beside you.

A primordial voice opens your inner ear.
You listen, rising and returning—
Back to the racket, back to the roar, into your current.

THE OTHER SHORE

Flow river, over velvet sands,
Around serrated boulders
Broken in the valley.

Slither river, like the serpent
Under and over the
Mountain's foot.

Live river, move with
Rushing, laughing motion in
Darkness.

Rise high river, fall headlong
Coursing with breathing buoyancy
After cloudburst.

Let us, river, cross over assured,
Leaving silver here to golden banks that glisten
The other shore.

LAST SEASON

Last season you left us, sailing off for heaven.
Eighty days. This vacant space
Has made so great a pain.

We peer across the street through two panes of glass,
Witness they've cleared trees to
Emptiness.

Few oaks still standing stand exposed in space,
Slim with thin limbs of green stretching into
Barrenness.

It will be many summers
Before restored in fullness.
Last season you left us, sailing off for heaven.

KNOLLS

Wobbly rocking knolls filled with yellow in autumn,
Where verdant green cedars point toward heaven—
Let's walk there awhile
In the shining—
Over there, over yellow lawns,
Over rolling knolls, into the yellow autumn.
Let's amble around in the emerald and gold where
The amber and emerald green cedars point like spires
Toward heaven.

IN THE HEART OF A HEATWAVE

In the heart of a heatwave
Of a Long Island summer,
We keep from heat in shadows of trees,
And sleep in the music of leaves,

Worn with the sweat of our souls
In blue viscous air,
We turn the earth with the shovel of hunger.
The Spirit hears our appeals and pleas

Watching over while
His wind lifts walls of haze
Between us away.
In sodden evening,

Under the roaring of thunder,
Safe from the quaking of the deep,
We awaken from tombs of our sleep.
In dew-covered morning

Calm on the shore after rain,
With the chorus of waves at the sea—
We walk together
Chained to the rhythm,

In the heart of a heatwave
Of a Long Island summer.

RECESSES OF A SUMMER

They hide in high black grass,
In dark green garden stalks,
Under the high hay stacks,
And cry through night, grieving
Beneath attentive stars.
We hear them—sorrowful,
Sad crickets.

And the moon, too, mourns,
Waning with tears
That pour
On old slabs of
Broken slate
Which lead the way we once walked.

THREE DUCKS

April's hills are teal and wet,
Dripping gray rain filling valley pools.

Bars of sunlight break, shattering
Shining glistening fragments over all that held gray.

Three ducks fly over Terrel River,
Calling, quaking calm silence.

DECEMBER WINDOW

Outside this window
The long gusts of wind whimper;
Winter tilts a gray face
To the earth.

Steady rain,
A lone swallow slips on the air to a tree limb,
Pauses, shakes twice,
Flies away.

LATE SPRING DOGWOOD, NEW JERSEY

In afternoon
A softened muffled wind,
A ripple of water, red-white petals in the air
Drop on the top of the pond.

Dusk, still wind,
Stars drip on the still water surface.
One cricket sings.
A dogwood weeps.

THE PRODIGAL

I mourned the day you left.
Gray sky, winter, still gull on a wharf post;
The horizon line blended into blurred mingling—
Sky and sea,
Uncertain confusion,
Ambiguous mist.
I watched your ship sail eastward
Inching toward Murray River,
Smaller and smaller.

CHRISTMAS NIGHT

Out for wood
I find the birches whiter by moonlight.
All's quiet, light, still and
Full with stars.

Inside
Voltage beams, mumbles, hums;
This moon finds no place,
This night no thought.

I'd like to stay, pray,
Or write a poem;
But it's cold and I'm only
Out for wood.

ARMS

It's graceful the way
The gray clouds climb
Carried by hands of wind
Over the ocean coast through stars

In the darkening far fields of the universe.
They're kept in the power of the wind,
As offspring in arms of a Father,
Not knowing the course,
Not knowing the cost,
Or where.

NOTHING EVER CHANGES

Blue jays scream; neighbors sleep.
Early morning's
Sun's blue hands hold you, and
The flow of cold water falls into soil
From the water can in your hand.

Like a child with cotton candy you carry upright
Lavender and lilac blossoms.
Water showers, mist leaps,
Light frames a rainbow—
Early May morning.

These remind us—nothing ever changes,
That our lives remain stable, still eternal.
Behind you in the high locust limbs the lofty air blows and moves
Swiftly as angels with scathing swords, flinging fragrance,
Tossing beige blossoms.

Stiff, sinuous, tapered limbs lean forward.
Pushes and brushes of breezes from the sea press against trees
And you; greenness lilts.
New buds of evergreens open in
Yellow palms of hands, and worship.

I watch you, my wife, your ardent movement as
You shine through lucid breakfast glass in green honesty.
Hair lifts behind you, shining aglow against white cotton
Contrast like petals of cherry blossoms
Against pastel expanse of sky.

Noon will come; the petals will fall, and summer will come.
Life will intrude with its revolution,
Its flurries of spores, organisms,
Sore hearts and old scores,
But nothing ever changes.

CLOUDS OF DAWN, WYOMING

The clouds of dawn march on the mountains.
They come synchronized, banging broken drums
While fingers of wind
Strum the strings of willows.

Swiftly water courses in the valley
Are filling and flowing with water,
While time, never flinching,
Cunningly rushes to some indifferent surface.

Noon shadows in vigilance
Languish in the meadows.
Sycamore twigs sharpen shadows
On green-black ground.

And all afternoon
The lucent face of the sun on swollen pools
Beams as the moon's
In night's peak.

MIDNIGHT

It's midnight, April, a quiet hour.
You've come alone to this blackness,
The edge of black woods.

Rainfall's drained. Pools and streams swell.
Water drips from still trees—
No blossoms, leaves, buds.

White clouds crack, split.
Blackness fills the cracks. Stars blemish blackness.
Small light from a window reaches out its warm hand.

The sounds that voice within blackness:
Peepers in the forest mere,
Ducks of the duck farm, dull hum of the Atlantic,

A car's wheels on a far rain soaked street,
Barks of worn dogs,
This dripping, your breathing.

You've come alone to escape your strapping wrestler,
    wakefulness;
Alone to escape your sleeping home, alone to meet with
    your forgiver
In the light of this raucous blackness.

DARK HOUR

A dark hour prowls forward.
Winter limbs scribble shadows,
Wave naked shapes in the wind.

Thick limbs *creak*
One lonely word over and over
Against a page of sky.

Cold, subtle flurries of snow
Fall. Dark barks of a fox rove
Over the low silence.

Jesus, You are the huge spruce,
While she at peace hides
Like a grouse in a bough.

VERMONT CEMETERY

Ice nestles in tire scars crossing grassy pastures.
Cold approaches early here—
As autumn throws gold on the ground.
It is dawn. Barn doors yawn. Steeples stretch.
Venus shines in violet skies.

We stroll behind this old church
Down a slope beneath maples
Where names and years of lives engraved
In slabs of stone like wheel scars in earth
Make rows and rows.

There's zeal that spears with jealousy holding back the
    plague;
That whips, that drives the animal out, turning tables,
A zeal that burns with burning fire,
That scars, marred more than any man's,
That cries to one creator.

A crow *caws*, flutters.
Tame wind blows cold up the slope.
Dead, brittle leaves rustle
Clustered like netted fish
Against the slender rows of stones.

DAYS

The days of oak buds pass by.
They shiver open, exploding over
Shadows of trees breathing.

Those early oak leaves wait in white
Like the feet of the unborn—
Fresh, unstained spaces.

In a moment shade lifts as sunlight
Shifts behind high clouds. The sound of wind
Dies, or sings acres away.

We talk of autumn, and see that we
Like oak leaves had walked over fields, so far,
Hiding behind tales.

We've tumbled out into light,
Humbled, aware that
The days of oak buds pass by.

PAINTING A HOUSE

On a Sunday I see from this roof
Puffs of blue smoke from cold mufflers:
Family cars leaving for church.
In the still of the distance the sea lies in sapphire,
A span of marsh land, cattails shining like ice,
December dry.

I recall Grampa's white hair,
Red weathered face urging, "Go to school. Become a doctor.
Become a lawyer."
He'd lean down, muss my hair, smoke cigars,
Coloring homes with cumbersome brushes,
Youthful blue eyes like the sea.

A quiet tide swirls, revolves.
Cold wind blows and shrills like violins in my ear.
Starlings dance over dead crabs, cluster like bees, leave
    ruffled.
Another thought, another shingle,
The melody of bells tolling in the village—
Months have drifted since I've visited God's house.

I blow breath through the narrow tunnel of my fist,
Slide down with palm and heels, slowly,
So careful not to spill blue on this roof;
I approach the tops of the ladder rails

Welcoming like open arms—
The safety of level ground.

TENSES

The moon's shining washes this present tense.
Its crescent rays bathe Moriches Bay
Whose waves paint the shore boulders white
And gray
Again and again.

The moon had joined us in the past
Perfect. It had been invited
Full and close
As it had risen over wide open spaces in
Trees, between houses, hills, clouds,
Possessing the purple nights.

The future moon will wane again, will covertly
Hide, will
Seep, smear, cover, rise,
Fall, will even become blood—not only in some poem—
But right here,
While the future perfect will have strode
Over Moriches Bay.

TREE FARM

At dawn songs of birds float across the tree farm.
Swallows dive
Down,
dart along the rows of yews, junipers, azaleas in scarlet
    orange.
A dim moon blemishes a blue sky.
One young doe within the openness—still, bright—
Rests in the first light of sun, grazing, gazing across
This place that is always filled with thick stillness,
Drowsing summer mists, winter frosts.

Once you searched here,
Lost in listening, longing to stay while
Sounds of storms swept inside your soul.
There are things that no eyes have seen, no ears have heard,
No understandings have understood—
things prepared for any who'll love
unforbidden fruit.

Now, in clamorous storms far from here
you find inside your soul
these summer mists, winter frosts, rows, swallows, fawns,
this tree farm, repose.

AFTER THE HURRICANE

The tide drowned the docks and high spiles,
And ducks just stepped onto grass.
We brought our bags of bread and fed the brown
Females, the green feathered males.

The wind wafted the heavy haze of September.
The sun fell red in the west
melting with yellow smudges
In trees across Orchard Neck Creek.

The power in town tarried all windy night.
The crickets of Moriches: thick, black,
big as frogs—
Gossiped in the gloom.

All along the southeast shore
In the wind pummeled, limb pummeled homes,
candles burned.
Some men slumbered when the light returned.

GREEN EYES

Thawing earth softens, swells,
Slips off thickness of winter—
Melts and strips this quilt of snow—sliding slowly
As though earth legs kick it
To the foot of the hill.
We sit before new glass at this window.
Gray driving rain chases wind
To corners. Moody Blues' music resonates
Carrying us back forty years.
Grassy holes disclose themselves through snow—
Green eyes peeking from frozen sleep
Through blurry windows of slush.

BRIDE

His eyes long to look upon his bride
more than all the color of the world,
Her wreath is sweet, fragrance sweeter
Than the favored season's breezes.
Her embrace like desert freshets
quench him.

His heart longs for hers.
She shines as light from sun.
He hears the supple sound of her voice.

Someday they'll enter gates, step on salient streets,
hand in hand in hallowed happiness,
in great white rays of light.
Their music—hers in His—
the harmony of stars
as they approach, closer.

FLORIDA SONNET

These clouds eclipse the sun out of our sight.
A gust! And now and then our sense can smell
A sudden glimpse which does not want to light.
It hides in hills of clouds that also tell
Of days at noon with breaks and open space
Which widen into whiter starry nights
That drip a silver gaze and heaven's trace
Like oranges, sweet oranges from heights.
These clouds eclipse the moon into the dark
Like fruit in limbs that hide within the shade
As we with thirst await beside the bark
For ripeness to come, for blossoms to fade.
It's the swollen, full fruit of sagacity
That falls like light with calm alacrity.

YELLOW MAPLES

What was once a place of darkness
On a day as bleak as this is, is
Now a place of lavish light beneath canopies of trees—
Spacious sugar maples whose limbs like summer bride's maids' are brown,
Wearing gowns of powerful yellow,
With trains at bare root-feet

spread on autumn's floor in yellow.
Poised inside like a bride,
Stands the slender fir posing in blue-evergreen
Holding a cluster bouquet of honey suckle vine,
Rising with quiet smiles
On her autumn wedding day.

These maples—yellow chatter,
singing the song of starlings
Deep within their hearts and throats.
Dark clouds come to darken;
these yellow maples brighten. Thunder comes tumbling
And windy rains pour and blow these

Starlings out from under these trees, and
Graceful thousands over green fields fly in formation.
They take their song, their dancing,
Leaving the sound of dull falling rain.
As rain still falls these tall maids cry.
As darkness falls, this blue bride sighs.

ICE STORM IN NEW YORK

The clock woke us to that ice storm,
Alarming the dark dawn to the cold. We were
Glad the yellow bus refused to roll over the icy roads,
That school would close all day.

Soon with the music of the first act
The sun burst, shoving aside cold rain curtains;
Then with the music of the second act
We came gazing in wonder at bright wet shining.

All glazed, dripping, clicking, sparkling sunburst,
The trees thought they looked best:
tall leafless ones wore radiant halos;
Birches nearly broken bent as birches do;

But the evergreens were beaten, bowed
Down with broken boughs, slumped like drunken men
Over fences, ice laden—hanging limbs
Swinging like arms in wind.

Such a menace of violence and crime:
We had our cameras at the scene.

OCTOBER HOUR

Sunless clouds lower.
Mounds of moss bulge above dead leaves
And needles—Soft springy cushions
Entangling roots of oak and pitchpine.
These are traces of jade
left to suggest last summer.

We pace. It is balmy.
We think we hear one weak cricket
in the middle of this woodland, somewhere
under what's rotting
speaking her words, somewhere.
We strain

with the sane same
patience we take when we shake out a last drop,
to listen, and wonder if we imagine,
Longing for all that remains
of the late stages
of summer.

TUCSON SAGUARO

Stone still and old as stars,
Some resemble men,
some the cross.

In April
Blossoms burst the tops
As fluids sop the womb.

Navajos
Long ago
quenched here.

Yesterday
I paced with an axe
Through the desert.

I chose one
And swung—*grunt!*
As if the thing felt pain.

A frail trickle ran
to the arid floor,
Long held tears.

MAGIC

Magic
Things like huge majestic doors opening
On thin hinges; plump penguins submerged, flying fast
Through freezing currents;
Like ponderous polar bears on water frozen
Over northern Manitoba;
like a man abiding
Forty years in God's forge—
Forged strong, sturdy.
Magic
Like the avalanche launched
Descending like white flocks
Falling to its place of rest.
Magic.

REMEMBER

Remember that night when water sang in the spring,
shined in the light of a moon where we abode in
a field of few words,
that night when summer stayed—
moon dressed in blue-white
one we didn't need to tilt our heads to see—
and songs of frogs along the creek
where we abode with
few words.

Remember that night when one piano
from one screened door
poured forth in the mossy mosquito night
for us.

You wrote and spoke a poem about a moon
unlike so many poems about so many moons
always broken and lonely.
Your moon was not lonely.

Remember that night when summer
felt like someone who'd come so near, so clearly blue-white
like the moon.

ORIOLE

You hear the call of the oriole from up atop the poplar tree.
Her arrival's early, moving March to May,
making us question
all our fury, all our hurry.

Her sure mate is far away;
She'll still wait for him. She'll still stay until
All of April's yellow frills fill the hillsides—
speckles over green.

I DREAMED YOU DIED

I stroll this street as
sleepless as three stars that
still pace the lanes of last night's rouse, lingering,
falling west.
In the east a green glow grows higher,
Gleaming brighter.

I dreamed you died.
I saw you gallop off
gallantly riding a white steed, deep into night, intent
toward a red crescent moon,
far on some unseen horizon line.
I thought you glanced back once.

I dreamed you died, and I grieved
leaping back into childhood grieving
rides we'd never taken,
crescent moons we'd never pursued,
horizons too far, too late, or too tired,
over all we wished could be.

You seldom gave your valued coins of time,
worthy things lost, not sought for,
ones years make priceless,
irretrievable.
I thought you glanced back once,
searching corners for those lost in dust.

I stroll this street as
sleepless as stars. Dawn splashes, rises,
washes the coast of all the filth of darkness past, casting
flakes of light on waves of gray,
painting them white
all the way to the horizon.

NIGHT OF A NEW MOON

I'm walking before a night of a new moon.
Winter is over the island,
dead wind and cold oak limbs
Above old hard snow on the dirt road.

I go alone, sleepy,
like the slow sun falling over the duck sheds.
I come to the field by the fishpond
Where water under ice creaks and gurgles
and snow dust swirls in the air.

Two moons ago
Goldenrod shone in the grass.
Earth and sky
Now drowns in winter dusk.

I go home slow
To hear in sleep
Sweet music in my skull
In a dark night
Of a new moon.

ORDER IN HAMDEN, NEW YORK

We are walking. It is evening.
The straight lane lies paved, painted
in fine white lines evenly spaced
like heart beats of time,
clock ticks of life.

We are walking. There is order.
Rows of growth growing green cover the world
like warranties in words on pages—

Broken Prose, Spoken Poems

food for a future—these green rows cross our vision.
It is August. Blossoms promise fat roots
hidden, caked thick in red clay, potatoes waiting for sun.
These rows of green consume our fields of thought which
    grow so wild,
flowering unruly.

We are walking. There is order. It is evening.
We seek the wild life—fox, coyote, snake—something
    slinking out in this quiet world's order—
something sudden—just wildly alive
to take us away from us,
from our tidy disorder,
someplace secret.

It is evening. There is order.
We are walking in the wonder
full of August silence.
We look upward for the hawk's flight.
We look to look like her in her high grace, her high eyes.
We look to soar the august skies, but
we are walking in our order. It is evening,
and we are feeling humid air, the humiliation of
    humanness, as
we come to the poplar hollow where the stream glides
    pliant and clear.
We are searching, finding slivers of fish, silent transparent
    forms, fish—
transparent as poplar shade above us.
They sparkle, dart away
beneath this clouded glass of shallow stream
to their own secret places.
There is order. It is evening.

ELIJAH

One who never did die
once prayed, "Let me die."
Later a flaming chariot arrives soaring—detouring
Flying farthest—answered ancient prayer.
He prayed fervently.
The swampy world is sinking, yet
We recall the scent
Spring will bring—prevailing on the breezes
of some Sunday morning when
"The sun of righteousness shall arise with healing in his
    wings"
here in this world's swamp.

BROKEN LOBSTER BUOYS

Broken free from their moorings by storm or lobstermen's
    slip,
They find them on these beaches—these buoys—
broken white spots
that dot the wide red shores
like stars the skies.

Fitting litter. Styrofoams once afloat. Traces of man's mess.
Light lovely irony. Those still whole with black loops
at round ends—
links to rope and trap—they take home,
scrape away seaweed mud, whitewash, dry.

Later with paint they make worlds of lighthouses, ships,
sails at sea, waves at wharfs, gulls at crabs,
shells and fish by cliffs and clouds; worlds
of nine mile horizons,
worlds of suns, moons, stars.

A safe escape, these worlds of curiosity
they create—free of litter, idyllic.
They could do much worse
than be painters of
broken lobster buoys.

APOSTROPHE TO TIME

Between these moon rays you hear—
A fox barking from somewhere in blots of darkness.
You sizzle across the sky in shooting stars
Audible to all.
You rise.
You fall in cycles of tides, in
Spinning circles in
Precision
Visible to all.
You wane through moons.
You fill moons
And march through months ascending heights of seasons.
You tick in clocks, throb in pulses, thump in hearts
Audible to all.
You are the unmasked thief of youth.
You steal years by fruitless pursuits.
We just watch you.
You're visible to all.

SHELTER ISLAND AUTUMN

Autumn on Shelter Island falls on small talons
Like wild birds crowded with color.
She splashes her life from her blue gulf
Smothering hastily last traces of lonesome summer.

We will wait until the last blush wanes, fades, ebbs
In the colorless dust of November.
It is over. Winter frowns, bullying his angry way,
Killing all color.

THE ROAD ABOVE THE RIVERS

This road above the rivers we've often ridden.
Its bridges crossing over those moving waters,
And we hear our muffled wheels rolling and reeling at
   speeds
Exceeding ninety.

This road we've often ridden sometimes speaks to us of
Ancient paths, paths natives have trodden. It tells us old
   stories of cold, ice hardened,
Old paths where strong ones once walked,
Strong Native Canadians
Emerging from tall teepees, full-feathered, ready.
"Keep your moccasins on the ancient paths," they were
   told.
"Keep your feet where your fathers walked. Keep your feet
Where your fathers' fathers fought."

We've been down this road before.
This road we've often ridden.
She recites her poems in measure and meter and never
Finishes her long, first nation lines.

Canada stretches her arms forward
Like a tired bear
Hibernating within the doors of ice caves,
Snoring, roaring, waiting for the first cracks of spring.
These rivers slither. They're veins finding the world's heart.

These rivers slither. Pulsing as arteries, packing their bags,
Leaving the land's heart.

This road we've often ridden
Above the slithering river.

POET

She's too shy for the stage—child playing make believe,
    plotting, putting
Attempts at truth on white in black defiled ink.
She searches for innocence, purity's sister
Through fallen confessions, confusions, and human sounds.
She's the shy hider behind closed curtains of hanging night,
Suspending silence, prosaically waiting,
too tone deaf to sing song lyrics.

She's a child whispering wishes, a strummer of words and
    wooden stringed shouts to worlds aloud.
Pigment blind, and can't find the right shade to recreate
    creation,
Your canvas sprawls as Kansas sprawls, in tense tans,
blemished greens.
Your tones of words whisper, babble, ramble and
Shift scribbles read through dark glass.
Your words are one brush strokes sprawling glorious tan-
    green grasslands,
Soundless canvas scars searching for innocence
And still life.

MARCH SNOW

Longed for March strolls into our Canadian field.
Her sweet scent, her cold clean snow, freshly
Fallen in clear air,
In midday sun
Melts.

Her brightness blinds us. She rises above
A dozen memories
Once frozen like dreams in sleep
Remembered. She shines
in our minds, smiles with eyes
Squinting. She greets
Us, and we breathe deeply
Her warm coldness, her dripping beginnings of spring,
Her dozen frozen memories—old, slowly
Melting.

March meanders into our field, whitens our world.
We're in our meadow of life where
In our meadow of life the
Sure sound of the foaming sea is heard afar, is
Heard in the depth of our soul's ear.

Winter's over. March climbs
Onto our Canadian shore with life, our island's curves,
    coves, and slender creeks
That reach like fingers
Inland, searching
For earth, full with dripping beginnings of spring,
Slow midday snow-thaw, with
Old memories
Melting.

POEM FOR YOUR 58TH BIRTHDAY

Away from you today again
The view from our wide front window—I imagine
How you see our street through sheets of rain
Puddle-full at the feet of trees, how
You wake to a jay's call, and pray
For one of ours who's far from home.

I imagine you move then
to the rear of our home
you've made right and kind,
Gaze through glass—our green-gray lawn,
Search for the jay that called, and pray
For a child of ours who's far from home,

Grown now, and we remember their
Running through leaves raked high as haybales
under the slanted massive swamp maple,
stumbling through its autumn orange,
Later in winter snow—
their quiet shouts in loud white silence.

Half our lives ago our dying child—
Beautiful baby girl—her blue death impression
Locked in our worried minds—
Corpse-to-be striving for life—
so onerous to behold, so hard
to give farewells.

Away from you today again
The view from my classroom window—
High above the breadth of high tech and books—
Brings my eye on a blue jay's dart into a maple.
I pray for you as you pray
For those of ours who are far from home.

INTRUDERS

They're dark, small,
Fallen angels some say the mad see as they
Scream in seas of confusion;
They're those that move us to cries for help.
Spring snow explodes in untimely

Thin silence, spilling thin winter—white, intruding.
The silver survivor—intruder—
Lone coyote loping over white fields,
Slowly, hungry.

We work words together in meter, build with syllables,
    prune intruders,
Puzzle musical pieces together. Words are sounds, sounds
    words,
Pieces of sense, senses of peace, voices of music without
    intruders,
Assonance recurrences, consonance recurrences.

Intruders,
The unwanted syllables,
Stunters of growth, sudden traffics, broken bones,
uncalled for callers in phones, clogs, spills, slips,
    bereavements,
Hurts in words, gestures in shoulders,
Grimace in faces, promise in frowns,
Infirmary hours, blood spills before sutures,
Blocks in roads, stops in clocks —intruders—
Steps down, leaps up.

GATHERINGS

Red sun rising over frozen ocean,
Sinking unflustered, slowly
Ticking, telling time.

Flocks of geese
Form formations in far fractions of sky
With destinations,

soar over lavender frost,
Their *honks* and *squeaks* acres away—cries—
Creation's urgencies, or calls

To porpoise pods in their purple struggles,
In their worlds of purposeful passages,
places of pain.

We people need each other, to hear each others' whimpers
In our gregarious creations, in our
Congregations of destinations.

TEREBELLUM SHELL

A conch,
A little augur
Shiny-slim,
Glossy—smooth,
Pacific shell
Sand dweller
In bullet shape
With short spire
In soft pastel
Wan patterns of
Sand colors, in shape
Like the pattern on
This thin page,
A subtidal find,
finished in time,
A piece of pretty
Death to cherish
And carry away
For keeps.

SAINTS

They descend into sleep,
The dream realm of valleys, dry streams
Filled with dry bones.

Fantasies rise as a phoenix
In white resurrection
From ashes,

In swirls of stars,
Swelling waters,
And foreign countries.

They awaken.
They brush off the dust
Of paltry death.

WAKEFULNESS

The broken empty bed of this life—

Before dawn you are awake.
The mosquitoes sing songs of their longings
Clinging to summer screens
With thirst for blood.

August darkness on Panmure Island hills—
The sky's bereft of stars; the moon's in bloom,
Blurred in vapors over the oval field.
An array of potato blossoms blazes.

Below your window—so close—
One cricket speaks.
From here you hear a lone coyote's cry
Far across salt marsh, farther across the bay—

His high pitch stretching westward
Piercing pre-dawn distance through silence
With thrusts of thirsting loneliness,
Reaching—I suppose—your soul only.

Wakefulness fills these rooms like squally wind.

Dawn begins to lighten this visible world,
permitting a quilt of mist, unruffled
To rest upon the land and sea, before

the empty broken bed of this world.

BLUEFISH

Sea swells endure in glossed forest green.
The sky lies glazed in gray.
Fine rain falls, spraying mist mixed with salt.

Fresh red speckles splash clots
In drops of bluefish blood, soaking the white
shining deck.

Bloody shoe prints smear—
Evidence in dances of violence.
They've fallen, all of them—

Fish buckets full—
To our deceitful lures,
Lost their sea-free lives

To devilish hooks, lines, sinkers,
Hungry human hands, knives, plates…
The struggle, the catch—

They rise above a surface of sea,
Ascend into death. Slimy tails slap.
Gills grapple for breath,

This ancient world
Continues its spinning, whirling
Imperfect balance—

Peculiar,
As on the spinning wheel
In the pottery barn.

SOYBEAN FIELD

The descending
compliant rows of green from mounds of growth
Between
low shadowed corridors, shallow valleys, narrow gullies—
A smooth view, a raked look, a soft growth—
The wind combs the soybean field
Turning leaves to successive waves all the way up
From the bay that is down
where the pink beach thinly
Cleaves
The two —the field and sea, the green and blue—
Asunder.
And then the crows' mewling *caws* are
Cloven
By ravens' cries.
To the east the mare of the crescent moon rises lemon
    colored—
Jaundiced—a hue somewhere
Between
The spectrum's orange and green.
To the west the sun sets
In egg yolk and red,
The tide rising, gushing westward,
The wind and waves pushing eastward, and we are
Descending
On bike pedals
Down the unpaved road beside the soybean field
Against the wind—prisoners for now to this earth, this
    life—both
Earth and life, so replete with
These betweens,
These asunders,
These easts and wests,

These subtle shifts in spectrums,
These tides that rise against the driven waves,
These that fall, and all
These contraries all full of views, hues, and rides
Down hill against the wind, and
up hill with the wind.

MILE FAR BONFIRE

We see this bright glow, hear its commotion—
intensity of light, singleness of sound.

A mile-far bonfire across a sprawling Illinois hill
From here a mere candle
Dulled and quelled by distance and darkness—
a mere murmur of burning through winter silence
In lulled muffled laughs—fire's noises, quiet voices—
A hallowed unity, a holy union—
Flaming laser radiance
Set apart
From cold.

Mile-far sparks fly upward into stars
The sure way starling clusters soar into wind.
Golden flakes of fire rise sending embers ascending
mixing in the Milky Way's hazed
Eternal soft fog, blend of blue-light wonder.

Beyond the fire the horizon lies east to west.
Trunks' and limbs' winter silhouettes
Hibernate in dormancy, stone frozen
Hiding in sleep, death's similitude,
Hidden, aglow by firelight—
promise of resurrection, ascension,
Light, life.

A NEW APOSTROPHE TO TIME

You're the grinless sheriff
Handcuffing my days
Into limitations.
Your prison cell
Like a shoreline:
Here and no farther,
Now and no further.

WATERFALLS

Rain cascades, slides to waterfalls.
Slivers of silver streams tinted sallow by a setting sun
Stumble down slipping
Sliding headlong
Into the long oval lake which loves
To swallow—chin lifted, head tilted
drinking—
all the water
Falling.

A TIME TO THROW AWAY

Search memory,
Rummage under rubble
In moth-balled cellar
Of yellowed past.
Dig out debris, dross,
Worthless odds, ends
Fit for the trash heap.
Toss them there to fester
In fires of burning forgetfulness
Forever.

Search memory
Carefully slide out,
Wash, polish, shine
Those items of returned desire.
Find the worthwhile pieces
For the window show—out, festive—
Show to those who remember tomorrow
The final fires of His refining
The crucible for silver.

THE SOUND OF WIND

When you last loved the sound of wind moving through
 trees—
God impelled—
Swiveling, whistling, whirling
Into the high limbs of winter,
Or strumming the willowy limbs of summer,
You were young.

Now you just listen to the fine-tuned gusts and
Wonder ,
What is it it utters to us, this wind?
The stronger the force the more mellifluous the lilt—
 music that lifts
like choruses, crescendos ascending in breakings of
 branches,
Then pauses, falters, softens.

When you last loved the sound of wind moving through
 trees—
God impelled—
Sent and loosened like light
Over water moving, roaring in whispers of winter,
Or whispering roars in summer,
You were young.

Now you just listen—
Invisible hands of wind caressing the surface of sea, and
Wonder what is it it intones to us, this wind?
The swell of a wave rises in silence,
Then falls, falters, crashing in breaking crescendo,
Like the breaking of branches, the toppling of trunks,
The brokenness of youth.

OPERATING ROOM

We wheeled you into that well lit whitened room
Where blue mask faces waited in blue aura
And Bronx darkness
Washed and scrubbed.
Hands held eye level scalpels.
We backed away wildly afraid, unable to gape.
We prayed through the long night
Far far from the sight.

BROWN TROUT, WOODSTOCK, NEW HAMPSHIRE

Brown trout glide with power, fly through water currents.
Sparrows swim through heavy air, and here we are
Seated beside this quiet
        Winding
Waterway,
Leaning, looking,
trying to see as trout would, or sparrows could,
held by chains of human weakness,
held by humanness.

FLEEING MOUSE

Fleeing mouse across the freeway leaps,
Dashing safely into sky-scraping weeds,
Then dances—we imagine—an
Innocent dance—puerile joy, having escaped
Unscathed—
As we prowl over, passing
On four power driven wheels
Speeding through Salina, Kansas.

HEAVEN'S DIMENSIONS

The mulberry tree bleeds
All over white pavement.
Heaven's heavy dimensions are mentioned—
Turn the page and see.

Elms potently plunge upward
Like fountains of living water.
Jesus, at your feet we sit—
Sixty years.

HURRICANE SANDY

While all spun above us
Houses cartwheeled under a moon
Hidden by clouds smacked about with God's scythe.
We heard the sound of many waters,
Wondered what the fish felt under a crashing crust of sea,
Remembering the fixed galaxy emblazoned
Across blackened spirals of the universe
While all spun in chaos just above us.

SNAKES

Snakes lurk, bark with snarls of rotwilers
Pitbulls, and wolves.
We speak your name, Jesus.
They turn—
tails between legs—
Lost, powerless
defeated hisses.

GREEN HOUSES

Emerald buildings,
Transparent iridescence,
Shells in symmetry—
God's vision through and
into thin human skins,
Symmetrical order—immortal
life residing within.
Limpid transparency
Pulsating greenness
Of life rising from wet, hot loam
All glowing through.

SUMMER FIELD

There's something sorrowful about the summer field.
His face sits in ignominy,
a shame of isolation
By the Prince Edward Island bayside.
Walk to the corner where the tractor turned a lazy turn,
Where the brush hog missed some young sprung saplings.
It's there—in the place of painful snubs and rebuffs
we hear a voice speaking with sureness
surpassing the suffering of slights.

GRAND DAD

Smoker of Lucky Strikes, loud laugher,
Man who used pliers to pull rotting teeth—
I still recall those ruddy blood clots spat
At the chipped, white, porcelain sink.
You didn't even bend your torso.
Old soldier, trooper with wounds,
You taught me—little kid—
to eat my peas without gagging.
"Mix em in the mashed potatoes!
Pepper! Pepper!"
You taught tough tenderness,
lived tender toughness.
Your broken poetic prose,
in my memory spoken
From a heart as vibrant
As Brooklyn, as big as New York.
From that toothless mouth you shouted
Into my little affected ears—
sardonically sensitively
Under the loud mouthed shadows
Of screaming jets descending to Kennedy:
"Don't be ashamed to cry! I'm not ashamed to cry!"
And you did just that, once glazing your face with tears,
"Some things make me cry!" you said with your New York
    lilt.
You cried when the Yankees won—watching grown men
Who'd triumphed in child's play—the leaping team like
    children
When the World Series was won up in the Bronx.

EVANGELIST

Fiery old preacher full of amplified fury,
Over-boldness blazing over the railroad yard.
Tall, tilted tent.
Plum pulpit
Flimsy in the field—that field that years earlier
Had grown something yielding, willowy, yellow—

Maybe barley, possibly wheat.

Old bard of coatless poems come in summer from afar—
somewhere in Canada, land of Midwest widths, to our small county's
Corner—come with loud life, flaming fists,
index fingers staring
Down
Our stony smoky souls, our adolescents drunk in beer,
Adults in secret sins, smoldering.

Here you hatch—bizarre bird chirping words, catching
Ears, eyes, us by surprise, evangelize
In flames of loving rage.
God. That angry? We wondered, squinting at sunset.
When the sermon's story closes,
Your homeless poem folds—you weep, weep, weep
feeling God's melted heart of fire.

SOMEHOW OUT HERE

Somehow out here on the lake shore
He makes us breakfast: baked bread,
Broiled fish—foot long rainbows—cleaned,
Seasoned with salt, basil, and bayleaves,
lemon basted,
Cooked over olive wood coals.
A dry swept morning.

Somehow out here from this little ship
Where we've drifted from our mooring, moonless and
Mourning, delirious and starless, weary
With rocking in labor and waves—nets filled
With emptiness—
He blends in in this yellow sun-soaked dawn unrecognized,
Far on the steady shore.

Somehow out here we know
Who this is in this familiar distance standing,
And we're drawn, dragging a sudden harvest, garnered,
Too heavy to haul to shore.
One plunges in in sudden swim ecstatic toward
The sure golden shore. Ours are faces of children
shining in tears before father.

How can we ever say,
"We're sorry" with all that we recall?
His steady gaze,
His cadent tone
Somehow out here
In the sallow washed-out dawn
Tells us He's forgotten.

WINTER HOURS

Fisted hands have held handles of axes.
Sinews have swung their heads
Down,
have lifted, split, and stacked
up in Canada.

We've counted the hours of winter,
Measured the nerves of trembling survival,
wondering on our wanderings
Between walls,
Worn, wearing shadows cast by deep true light.

WAITING

Can't help but scribble little words while she waits for You God,
Can't help but write words this night, words while she waits
 for You.
She can't help but speak to You from these fields of words
Of weeds she wants pulled
from the soil of her heart.
It's Your words she gulps down—
those fixed in stars, always filling the vacant places out there
Within her.

WAKING FROM A DREAM

Within a dry July night
Our clock ticks its black rhythm.
Skunks poke noses through thick clover searching for grubs.
We rise from sleep as shallow as eyelids, dreaming of
Our dying father.

He is young, in this dream, chasing us in earnest seeking,
 calling—
His voice, our names.
We're running from him—a convolution of hallways,
doorways,
alleyway mazes,
weaving
Through our childhood parish—all a fallen,
broken confusion.

For decades We've been hiding
Behind walls of words, joke making,
shielded smiles, cordial laughs, gates of silence, knowing
From ancient scripture—
Wisdom whispers blends of truth with love.

Broken Prose, Spoken Poems 51

We arrive here
To these hours, Dad's death, evening,
A hallway light—
Fresh wrinkles in midnight's mirror—
Old foresworn sins elbowing our ribs.
Garrulous guilt grows, yet we know of the irony
in God's great blood that bathes, makes
White as wool and snow.

Flip a switch on the back porch.
A flood lamp chases darkness and skunks—
Their black bobbing across gradual darkening, across
Grassy clover and black-green.

God, between us—us and you—
A stench of skunk,
The soft moss grown sound of surfacing rain, a sky of dark
    glass,
One open hole where a cluster of stars sparkles like ice—
Our cries ascending through.

SIX INNINGS

In our over-the-hill fifties
We drive west in the pick-up—
Radio baseball spoken motion through speakers—
Midday summer sounds are whispers.
Air whirls in the small world of the cab—
Wind through open windows.
We've finished six innings—
This pastime we call life.

Cumulus clouds like mountains mushroom upward.
They fill the sky in the south—mounds of pillowy white—
Shadow colors, shades of coal-gray.

The open road sends reminiscences—
Yearnings for yesterdays, tomorrow's longing—
The sun breaks, sends its streaks,
visible flashes of moving light.

Invisible wind—the treasures of heaven
Blow through hidden straws of angels, billowing
Over yellow fields of winter wheat.

We've finished six innings—
This pastime, this game.

BRIDGES

One stretches long across the sprawling width of water, nine miles
Conquering the width of Northumberland Strait,
Connecting whole Provinces: New Brunswick and Prince Edward Island—
Structure strengthened in mortar, human construction stretching
Engineered in girders and pilings conducting people who've purposes.

Another's
Small boards
Fastening
two forests,
Making one,
Crossing thin stream—
Black slither of
Water winding,
Splitting a forest
in two in pink
dawn darkness
over winter snow
languished in blue.

Bridges—
Connecting rods sending power,
Ancient aqueducts conducting water,
Red threads tying two
broken worlds.

The bridge-trestle traversing Long Island Railroad trains
Over Montauk Highway in Sometown, New York
Broke last year—severed—broken infrastructure,
Divorced, cutting the marriage of two townships.
Nothing to do but rebuild, strengthen, consume time,
    reconnect.

SEA SIDE

Our pace changes on a day by the sea side—
Umbrella colors in yellow air
Follow cloud shadows
Shoving blue aside with
Rude shoulders.
Clouds move over,
build room for sun, then
Crowd him out again.
Frisbees fly freely. Kites fly tied.
Flamboyant balls flurry above
Sprawling water—lucid, white, strident—
Below outspoken floating gulls.
One long brush stroke of human voices blended with
    waves,
The rising tide, the falling tide,
The sun's striding across the steadfast sky,
Youthful white clouds dodging time.

ALL AFTERNOON

Mauve southbound clouds move through blue heavens
All afternoon long. Their flickering shadows
Fall face down on the Ontario
Hay field—ghosts of decades gone.

That same wind as through these spruces whispers, pushes.
Evergreen boughs are sprung from trunks,
Trunks sprung from roots anchored—
Networks meshed, woven, rooted in sour ground.

These boughs, as arms
Bow,
waving farewell to clouds and shadows
All sunlight long.

MAINE CHAIN LINK

The creator's fingers set far away and neatly
The lake where it lay for our full view—
A puddle between three mountains—
Rain and gravity's rendezvous,
Fastened sheet of fragile glass,
Still waters holding frantic life

Hidden underneath, unseen
In dim depths of green.
It's where the lake trout fans fins,
And flurries his sturdy tail
In round turns and with no thought
In soundless swarms of slow circles

Intent in instinct, in hungry creature searches.
We wend our way down the winding
Sloping path pacing
Making space from our place in these hills,
Rods and reels in ready hands—
Intent in instinct, hungry savages searching.

TIME TO PRUNE

Promises, a month of Mondays—
Moon phases—some nights never seen, just
images imagined, predictable shapes—
Those phases—hidden as we hear rain and
Clouds winged by wind.

One waning gibbous Monday the gardener pruned.
We found a little tree standing handsomely. Look!
It appeared; never noticed. Then time
Permitted vines to climb, overwhelm,
Drown its life under.

Removals of strongholds, choke, foot, and other holds,
Grips of grim death—those severe severings
In our lives—hurtful prunings
Helping us love God in death of self—
Even in pain.

PASTURE

In the west the sentinel Venus sits. He is alert.
Tired old crescent moon reclines, leans back on his rocker
Reading in the den of dusk's east. Down here
Windy beeches and windy birches bow at the field's edge.
In the middle, one lone elm lifts limbs heavenward—
    maestro
Leading the trivial trees—giving homage in symphony.

The playful calf—she comes to me
Like a grandchild with nerve
Wearing little grin—I imagine—and
Little skip. This day—sweltered
With counting and human labor—
I almost forget how to play.

AMERICAN KESTREL

Neighborhood bully,
Bird of prey shoulders his way—
Loud killer of small birds and mice,
Falcon mimicry,
High perched perimeter watcher,
Dalliance diver, searching,
Screeching in flight
On Panmure Island.

Demanding notice at the air show
Four came to our field for summer.
The hummingbird feeder full of nectar—
The hummingbird fears keep them far.
They hear the kestrels
from dark forest shadows.
They hide from mean kestrels,
Those neighborhood bullies.

FLASHES OF MEMORY

We revisit with inner eyes memory flashes
All in sunlight, all in color—green and blue.
We hear the harps of years in the far heart of song,
Softly sung in our ears.

They smell the scents of summer sent from the sea,
feel fingers feeling fingers, and
taste the taste of fowl and fish
At tables firmly fit—

Decades into the well lit rooms
of memory—
Green eyes gazing into blue,
blue into green.

Children, labor, sleep, sighs, sips, cries,
Senior citizenship, storms, films, photos,
Phone calls and phone calls unreturned, unheard—
Even eighty years—

A flash, a year, a day that vanishes as a vapor
That seems to never end, but ends a vapor
all for something
"eternal in the heavens."

DAUGHTER

I've favorite unforgotten remembrances—
Your birthday, for one, as vivid
As an hour ago, holding you in your first mantle,
Speaking meekly, repeating your name.
Your cries subside, finding
Your breath, more breaths,
giving one little infant grin.
Other unforgotten remembrances—
Your beaming birthday face
and Christmas cracks of dawn…
And those drives, just us, long talks
To college, once lost by New Bedford,
But feeling fine if the drive took days.
Time with you, rest from life.
I remember your wedding day,
Your beaming wedding face.
I've favorite unforgotten recollections
Collected in thirty-four years.

BLUE BROKEN MUSSEL SHELLS

They shine on the wet shoreline—
Blue fool's gold for sea glass seekers
Who search for the piece of great price—
The blue, amber, red piece of sea glass—
The shard of farther history,
The painful traces, slivers of another time,
Wound makers healed smooth, softened by sea,
Fully colorful. You can spot them,
the sea glass seekers, that is.

They slowly stroll in bare feet, heads bowed
Crouching searchers. Bend, reach, lift, look—
They learn they've been lured by a beach devil's deceit,
Crustacean skeletons—
Blue broken mussel shells—
From the ripples of man's first fallen brokenness,
When he was sought for by Him who valued him who was lost in
Flimsy death, the remains.

The strong fingers of storms and tides comb, comb,
And comb again, raising old sea glass from beneath time's sand—
The weighty stones sink and frivolous
sea glass rises, repeats rising, to their shapely colors,
The pellucid to pearly white.

Transparent lusters appear
Above the crystals of quartz, gravel, and stone—
Gifts from the past, the human past.
Fingers excavate, sort, search. Nothing resurrects them like
The combing of the sea—the tide,
The storm, combed through smooth—
Soft shards of thousands of yesterdays,

Even a hundred years—shards separated from shells—
Preserved ruins of the labors of man,
Old ocean worn, sea broken glass.

THE PAST

Memory, the past.
The sound in a scent, the touch of a sight,
Something subtle touching some sense—
A taste in time suddenly brings me there—
Down
Dragged to those
sunken stones
At the bottom of the sea
Where vivid words are chiseled, still images.

Memory. The past.
Just a song, or a scent,
Something soft touching some sense—
Four chords suddenly brings them here,
clear, up from depths with sounds of stringed instruments
Pumped up with air to breathing surfaces, clear,
Then higher in air farther to clear heavens—
Hot air balloons bursting,
Rising full with color.

Memory. The past.
We search pages for an old page of pain,
The weighty warm ache of memory,
A photograph, an old stone,
An unforgotten gist,
an ache of pleasure.

BROKEN POEM

The
Broken poem
That lolls in free verse excuse
For broken rhyme scheme,
Broken meter and all the word order patterns
That make our world orderly
Is just simply broken, unfinished, always
Saved to work on on a later day
When there's time or eternity to make
Unbroken, fixed, finished in redemption.

The
Broken stuff—
Are they still stuff? A
Broken bike is still a bike.
Broken heart, dream, promise—
a heart, a dream, a promise still.
We walked through gardens on broken slate,
On walks of broken boards, sturdy
With strong legs and good boots,
And we're broken.

The
Broken humans
Hurt, unhealed, harrowed, plowed
Before the seed is planted, or water poured—
Asleep in deep sleep on broken beds
Snoring, dreaming broken dreams.
Broken beings broken by beings who are also
Broken—some by unseen demons—
souls afloat in a world that is broken,
Fallen, stolen, waiting for redemption.

NUMBER SIX DREAMS

Number six sticks on my old jersey—gold over purple—
That dream recurs in color
In green fields, yellow goals in white frames,
yellow cards in handballs, near scores
that never splatter the back of the net.

Number six dreams—
Broken dreams, broken hope,
Muddy slumps in autumn losses,
Fast passes, long crosses, headers, traps, tackles,
Lone walks to buses, limps to lockers, hobbles to showers,
Lumps, bumps, hidden whimpers.

Dreams, wearing number six, where
Goalkeeper's saves made in dreams in fields of sleep—
Dreams where you never get there, can't finish,
Never reach your search—*thumps* of balls on far posts—
Almosts. Goals always only almost.

Dreams, wearing number six,
Dreams in drab disappointment,
Obstructive foilings, hindered, impeded—
Heavy rains on game days—lose by one—
The spotted ball, round dice flying, opposed, blocked,
    closed—

another almost—
number six, one shy,
only almost.

CONDITIONAL LOVE

The consummate oxymoron—
The conditional love fastened to hate—
Heated and basted in hatred—
It's the painted face, the hidden rust,
Termites unseen in the cellar ceiling.

You said you'd come back to me if….
And then there was silence,
The hatred of cold conditions,
The lostness of loose promises,
The slammed door, the self's demands
The bolted lock, the lies,
The tantrum.

What more could He relinquish?
the donor with no conditions?
With thorny coronet, bloodied beardless face,
Carrying curses, lashes, betrayal,
Slanders, dishonor, and worse
with a cross?

SPOKEN PROSE

I

Teach us to pray.
We seem to learn best about praying when placed in
Arduous places,
Hopeless places—places that remain hopeless without Him—
Places only He undertakes ably,
places calling for prayer—these places
Teach us to pray.

Broken Prose, Spoken Poems

We are fallen creatures.
We can't rise without our creator, without praying,
calling His grace, forgiveness… Him.
We're stuck under slimy stones
Away from our Creator.
We are fallen creatures.
The Lord's model is the cornerstone,

The great foundation to build upon:
"Give us this day our daily bread":
The great synecdoche for all we need—sustenance to
    live—
"Give us all we need to do your will!
Give us that bread."
The Lord's model is the cornerstone.

"Forgive us our trespasses
As we forgive those who trespass against us."
The river's frozen without forgiveness.
Forgive! There's no survival in living short of forgiving
    crimes,
No movement, no horizontal health, no vertical breath.
We forgive.
"Forgive us our trespasses."

"Thy will be done."
A far goal line, a massive waiver.
Praying is getting in God's line, placed in our places
Underneath His gentle gavel. Praying is not pushing,
Squeezing, jamming
Into our corner, our maker,
underneath our will.
"Thy will be done."

II

"Be anxious for nothing,
but in everything by prayer and supplication,
with thanksgiving,
let your requests be made known to God;
and the peace of God,
which surpasses all understanding
will guard your hearts and minds through Christ Jesus."
Philippians 4:6,7

Paul the Apostle's pen to friends:
"We wanted to come to you—even I, Paul—time and time
    again, but Satan hindered us." —the sole
    scripture—the sabotage of Paul's good plans—
not imputed to God's direct barrier.
Other barricades fold him under the Holy Spirit's
    forbiddance—
To go here, to preach there.

"Lest I be exalted above measure (by the many revelations
    of heaven)
A thorn of the flesh was given to me…
Three times
I pleaded…cried…requested…"
God's return? "My grace is enough…
My strength is made perfect through weakness."
Lowering, for those who pray,
When we or ours are broken.

Our Father permits our enemy to punch, thump, cuff us—
Our enemy bound to Father's will,
ignorant of his undesigned strengthening of
The Father's children.
Nothing afflicts
Beyond our Father's nod—His
Permission granted. Our prayer persists:
Thy will be done. Hinder our will.

III

In Israel's history, "They lusted greatly in the desert,
And tested God, and He gave them their request,
But sent leanness into their soul." *Psalm 106:13,14*
A steep price to pay—
When we pray, Our will be done.

God authors disappointments,
Pens our difficult stories,
Molds our painful quarantines,
Forges our links of chain,
Piles upward the mountains we climb.
He carries us over His higher purposes:
Our journey, the light at our feet—
His likeness. Our destination.

"I know the plans I have for you…a future…a hope."
   Jeremiah 29:11
He gives what's noble: a thorn, a thwarted plan;
And it's there we learn He meets our need, gives our daily
   bread.
"Whatever the Lord pleases He does." *Psalm 35:6*
I do what I will, but still
I want your prayer, part of my plan.
Trust me with all your heart.
"Lean not on your own understanding."
Acknowledge Me in all your ways.
I'll direct your paths.

IV

God answers Job's questions with questions.
His broken world broken apart: kids, health, wealth killed.
He pleads, receiving peace that transcends understanding.
God's queries answer queries. Job surrenders,
"I spoke of things I don't understand, too wonderful for
   me." *Job 42:3*.

Job gets it. We get it. What?
The idea that we don't get it.
Your will be done. Your ways are higher.
You know what you're doing. You do what You will.
You want us on board. You rest in the boat, at peace in the
 storm.
We're going to the other side.
You said so.

V

Jesus prays, in skirmish with His humanness,
to His Father at the edge of the end.
"Let this cup pass from me. Nevertheless, not My will, but
 Yours
Be done." Staring down the cross,
He prays, entreats His Father, knowing
His limit without Him.
He never knew the day or hour of His return,
Never knew who'd sit with Him
In His kingdom.
He learned obedience through His suffering.
He learned dependence on His Father.
Lived in the power of submission, the Father's will.
Not until His triumph over death He proclaims,
"All authority and power in heaven and on earth has been
 given to me."
And He gives to us, as we yield to Him, to do His will.
Face to face with Pilate, "You would have no power over Me
 unless
It were given to you from the Father above."

SOD FARM MEDITATION

Kelly green leaves of grass by the trillions
make velvet carpet verdant for acres
As far as eyes see.

Tires of tractors roll.
Forks of hi-lows load.
Beds of trailers haul.

Grow them here; move them there.
We walk in a world that shifts and swirls.
We crawl on earth that quakes.

Anchors stay; transplants change.
The floor of ages shifts.
Leaves and mortals come and go,

Enter, exit.
Kept vows keep promising.
Betrayals stay extant.

To and fro, fast we go,
Bearing bags of seed, carting tears in flasks
To scatter here, broadcast there.

Shallow roots suffer
unheard
Until our welcome home.

SILHOUETTES AT SUNSET

Sunset seethes in the western sky—
fire aflame in sleek ribbons streaking across space,
Tangerine tinge.
Silhouettes of evergreens on the periphery of hills,
of limbs and drizzles of twigs
lingering through placid black shadow-lands
where we sojourn.

We listen all life long
To tunes of silver-tongued fowl—
The watchman owl, lovesick nightingale—

All nightfall long.
Forever in seminary, it seems,
Always learning to—"count"
through diverse trials,
in refining fires—"it all joy" probing
For gold in glaring glory
Somewhere at the end of the open road.

Dawn rises above hours of sleep
to her feet, and
We'll rise to ours, stride as
roaming pilgrims
holding closely the trail guide's rope, lifting
Fellow visitors who faint along the way
wearing shoes that never wear,
Ever sure to get there.

SITTING

Sitting. Just sitting.
Sit still! Stay put!
Days pass. Weeks, months…
Still sitting, waiting through
Days. Be still. Learn to be still.

Study in sitting, in stillness.
Just sit still in the mystery of stillness,
In the cushion of fallen quills of running time.
Wait. Wait in the court room
Of the planet. Sit. Wait.

A lark sits on the gutter guard,
With creased wings folded closed.
Time descends its vertical slide
With paws of patient speed
And legs of swift patience.

The sun rose in tints of rose
And fell in hues of yellow.
Her face smiled; her mien frowned.
A lark sings on the gutter guard,
With creased wings folded closed.

SNOWFALL AND WOOL

Sin's strewn like satellites of cancer—sickly reddish
Gnawing all surrounding cells,
Strewn like crimson debris shivering
In cold, frozen interstellar space
Across exposed expanse,
The galactic barrier of planetary void.

It spreads itself scattered
Littering a scope of cityscape—
An ugly dispersion of filth
In scarlet lots of scraps: old tires, broken fixtures, broken
Blocks, rusted bikes, cracked plastics, worthless drivel,
    wasted
Gibberish, rubbish, junk, just brokenness.

"Let us reason…" a voice of grace.
A woolen mantle in warm white layers slides
Down, descending, covering the reaches of red
dark universe—congenial, relieving. Snow drifts down in
    thickness,
in soft widths of whiteness—snowfall
covering, smothering ugly sin.

A VAPOR

I hear a human voice, lyrics, Neil Young
harmonica, piano, strings in song.
They all thrust me back thirty-three years.

"What is your life?"

I smell the smell from a pan frying fish.
I'm back farther, grandma's kitchen.
I'm seven again.

"It is only a vapor."

I see a pretty Chevy 63' pickup, blue,
parked on Parkside.
Swiftly my mind revisits its time.

"It appears for a little while and then vanishes"

Whoosshh! What was that?
flashbacks of places gone, your life my friend.
Can I do that over?

"away."

Honks of geese soar overhead, pass out of sight
Southward like gentle jets,
Never to be seen, heard, felt again.

GALVANIZED BUCKET

My galvanized bucket
Lasted long—Decades.
She hardly rusted, remained hard,
A hard to crack
Or puncture vessel.
That pail held water,
Kept the heat of shoveled embers
From burning our world down.

Somehow
in her old age she
faltered onto the thruway of
the driveway,
Compressed, perishing
In sardonic sudden death.

She's planted in the garden
Full of soft soil, with
Tulips, hyacinth,
And daffodil bulbs—
Memorial for
A faithful servant.

EASTERN NEW MEXICO

Eastern New Mexico, replete with emptiness;
Like sprawling parchment postponed for words,
A vast canvas waiting for paint—
Purposeless spaces of austere expanse,
Parched width, scope of sky
And hues
Lies before us,
so business-like
with bulges, bumps like warts on skin.
The open road bursts ahead, splurging
Westward into sprawling vastness—New Mexico—
Onward toward the frowning smiles of our futures,
Forward toward a scrubbed flat morrow,
Like sprawling parchment postponed for words—
The secretive likelihoods of our lives.

FISHERS ISLAND FERRY VIEW

The sky's an upside down sea:
Low curling clouds cling to cold slow winds,

Crumpled stratus clouds resist, remain fixed, above.
The ferry rocks. We remember

we watched you walk toward your truck
Over the lot's black blankness,

Alone, unlike
These couplets—

Alone, like this lone line—

Diagonally freely across the fused
White-lined well-ordered open-ended squares

Painted straight and tidy for cars'
Parking order, so like those confining

"Fill your name in the empty spaces provided"
Guidelines for the applications:

Tomorrow's hopes, impending prospects,
Possible promises.

REBUILD

One year beavers conspired to build their lodge
At a dipping bend in the Sturgeon River.
They labored with and without patience—
arm in arm with the steady obstinacy of time.

Their dam did what dams do, jamming the flow,
shifting the river's route. These mammals felt well
In their modern dam, but flooded
A riverfront human home.

The humans became compelled to rebuild,
Raise their foundation
Arm in arm with the steady obstinacy of time, until
They were pleased, beavers pleased, river pleased.

Years passed. Great rains came on the lax back
Of three feet of snow. Water like wet earth surged
Crumbling the dam. The river found its former course.
The beavers, compelled to rebuild, began.

THE PARDONER

He wanted to be the executioner, one
Who ties the knot, hanging hoods over shamefaced faces,
Or one who opens the gallows'
Trap door
Dropping the culpable
Only so far—before the floor.
He wanted to be the executioner, one
releasing volts, gas, guillotine blades, one
lighting the fire, one
driving the nails.
He wanted… until he dreamed he saw himself—
Mirrored stare as he swung from the rope,
Nailed, wired, ported, peering into the bottom
Of the French basket,
Beneath the guillotine praying,
Guilty.

He wants to be the pardoner, the carrier of keys
Unlocking gated locks,
Following orders of a justice—righteous,
Who sets the captive, guilty,
remorseful free.

INDIANAPOLIS

Interstate lit by high
lights snakes around
limits of Indianapolis
where human race lives—
mystery city, modern
ghost town of the
impious late hour—
semi-skyscraping
downtown in space
age aura—blue neon
rectangular crowns,
structures aglow
in light blinking
summer haze like
rocket ships within
the final countdown.

Long spinning hours of darkness recline behind our tired
    tires
As far as Columbus, Ohio; even farther east.
Pleasing welcomed lights of Indianapolis ignite
this small corner of the measureless Midwestern night
daubing darkness's fourth watch in lofty mauve-blue.
Beneath the starry depths of the universe this infinitesimal
    city—
This Indianapolis—reposes like a spark, a small waning
    campfire—
The last embers aglow in one small campsite in the
    immeasurable cosmos.

THE BELFRY TOWER BELLS

The belfry tower bell
Sends its song along the city lanes
Calling all who'll come.
The sounds resound
across the windless fields
far beyond the urban lanes.

In humid midsummer,
In frigid midwinter
The belfry tower bells
"into the highways and hedges,"
Compel all, "Come in…
that the house might be filled."

GREAT HORNED OWL

A still sun peers into cold dark depth of woods,
Into reeds down trails that swerve
And coil
along the river, wandering
Into marshes along the bay.

Midday tide slides low and sun peaks high,
shining, spreading gold over silver shoals,
over a gray surface of the inlet from the bay.
The laurel leaves curl in the cold bred by the solstice.
Up the sandy trail the constant calls of crows cluster in the
    high limbs
Within the shelter of winter trees,
Where one wide great horned owl launches
From low perch on silent wings—alone, away
From badgering black crows, evading
Trunks of trees in

low, silent flight, maneuvering
swift colossal grace
like a slithering snake,
Escaping.

Exquisite sacred bird—
Weary, wearing scared confidence in suave posture
Wearing strange hate in sinister eyes as old as a devil's, head
Melded in bloated shoulders,
swiveling,
watching with feline eyes,
Hissing, hiding fear in the guise of wide shoulders,
lifting the thick weight of darkness in the forest.
She clicked her bill in the winter stillness.

Was it some stolen carrion that made the black scavengers
    furious?
Something this hunter killed that had them uproarious?
Was it sleep these crows from this owl stole?
What rendered this stalker so helpless?
What made this darkness dweller bewildered in light?
What made this victor of night a victim of rickety birds of day?
In gold-gray glare of solstice light,
The great owl fled from limb to limb shrieking in weakness.
The winter had bitten in, ice gripped as the sun
descended in fields like flocks,
In woods and freezing inlets of creeks and bay
Where deciduous trees freeze,
And long brown grass lay matted
under thin broken icing of snow.

Trunks, limbs, twigs of oaks become scribbles in black
Against yellow glow of the fiery fall of day.
This wilderness
Like the human race is
crowded gardens of darkness.

Tree trunks are torsos, limbs arms, twigs fingers,
So many hands reaching for light.

The icy sky grows far and clear. Stars poise
Nearer than a crescent moon
Hanging within the limbs,
Swinging as a pendulum, waning.
Constellations dance as though on a stage of the earth's
    edge
Across the falling distance in fields of darkening skies.

STOVE FIRE

Indoors in the stove we build fire
Where roaring sounds grow loud like wind,
Flames blaze, thick strips of locust bark sizzle,
Kindle, snap sparks up from sun red embers.
From trunks of old oaks we drop chunks
Like bulky stones,
Down deep
Into the breathing, coughing chest—
this cast iron stove.

Smoke blows through, up the flue from the smokestack
Fogging sky, hiding stars.
A restful sound sounds a distant singing in the slow hours
    of burning
Where white wood reduces
to ashen ashes
in blue flames
waving, fanning upward, whistling,
Snapping muffled—pronouncing words
we've never learned.

SNATCHED

Six of you as babes we snatched
From dirty rooms and smoky streets
Of Addis Ababa and Brooklyn,
Seoul and South Bronx
Where birth mothers birthed you.
We washed you with water and love
Beside the watercourse among
Water lilies, watering you with
Firmness and blemished nurture.
We limped along in broken limbed
Imbalance, shortfalls in coffers,
Weariness and sickness,
Blue-collar toil in grueling hours.
Now we find you in front of facebook,
Screen games, and phone screens,
In university halls, soccer, baseball
And other fields; changing your
Offspring's diapers and tantrums,
Following your own unruly rules,
forgetting scripture verses
We ordered, rewarded you to learn.
We pointed and pushed
You in the route we ourselves
Had somehow by fluke luck,
divine providence—blindfolded
Found in our youthful lostness—
In the shadow of the cross of
Our high hero, Jesus Christ—
Having been lost in a lost world
Ourselves—but snatched ourselves
From dirty rooms and smoky streets,
Placed in the safe place of honest
flawless promises.

SON

When you were a child—
small, scared, tired—
You clung, crying, "Piggy back Daddy!"
We'd play—little knuckles against my throat, legs draped;
Or seated on shoulders, high, so close.

And when in deep snow I stepped short steps
So you could follow, pintsized legs fell in like posts:
"It's easy when I go in your shoe-holes Dad!"
You'd raise high knees, find foreseen prints,
learn to unburden your walk with your Father.

"Follow me as I follow Father,"
Was the chant; then you grew to that interval when
individualism found independence,
until, at best you followed at a distance;
at worst, got lost.

REJECTION

It shades in hoary grays—
Shadows in ashen gloom, overcast
As in the unreturned "Hello."

You're unfit for the shelf,
Not worth the work, rework,
Any renovation, reconciliation;

Unfit for the attic,
Amiss, out of tune, missing strings, keys,
You're remiss refuse.

Distressing message
Found in a bottle afloat,
"We're sorry but… we regret to inform you…"

The college, position, proposal,
divorce, denial, door slam,
Unanswered mail—

It shades in hoary grays—
Shadows in ashen gloom, overcast:
As in the returned "I don't want you."

POETRY

This careful language laced in grace,
Antiphonal tongues in lines in lyrical tones, in
cadence-sense,
in sentences—
What is it it recites to us
spelled in blood-ink spilled into printers?

Orderly violence lancing language,
Order drawn from order,
Sought out in babel, ravel, fog—
Pattern in sense's sound and sound's sense—
highest antithesis, supreme antipathy—
Shards of words like broken jars in the potter's shop—
reassembled, discarded, renewed in
hands on clay at the wheel, watered with tears
Healing, spinning fresh vessels
And vowels.

This laced language—what is it it leaves us?
Like water waiting lukewarm in
Sounds in the cellar heater reshaping cold to hot;
renovation of plain prose purposed toward perfect verse,
always a *nearly*, only an *almost*—
The dragged net of fish to shore,
their flapping life in dying.

Broken Prose, Spoken Poems

This careful language—what is it it sings to us?
the finer part fitted for the finer site,
The tuning in the keys,
Restoration of a broken soul,
Health to broken hearted, words mended in wounded
    clauses,
recurring symbol in a still image—the mower
in a field made green since a month of snow melt.

This cadence—what is it it declares?
precise lines on pure white pages—
Final shining draft—polished smooth sophism,
Lovely language made lovelier
Like magnolias in May,
Conversion from death to life;

The soapy sound found in a scent of sense,
Untarnished touch of snowfall
Fallen to the coat of a wolf,
Or the yew twig's touch to human skin,
Or the tart sarcasm in the taste of tea leaves,
Labor of pain, pain in labor—

The fitting antithesis, the fleeting antipathy.

This sense in sentences—what is it it sends us?
The plummeting axe to chunks of unsplit oak,
Photo shots of words and shreds of sentences,
Perfect pictures in film of the familiar
Stuff of living;
It's the newer view in mourning, the bluer fields of
    morning.
It's the shaven face of phrases pruned, worked, reworded,
    rephrased.
It's pure moonshine obscuring the sight of stars.

THE OCEAN OF GOD

Surging heaves of house high waves roll
And leap atop each others' backs—
Whitecaps like pugnacious wrestlers in
Wind gusts rushing in furious rage,
Roaring enormous reverberations—
A tempest at its vilest!

Under this turbulent fury,
four fathoms down in
the ocean of God
sea creatures full with peace hide without fear;
thin fish swim at rest—no dread in serenity;
All's still, tranquil.

CLEVELAND, 28 MILES

Colors and waters of rivers—
Vermillion, Black, Cuyahoga, Huron—
Meander rambling, wayward turning,
All flow to the open palm of Lake Erie,
slowly downhill north.

On gentle swells of hills that roll to waves of this great lake
Between these rivers
Orchards in ordered rows sprawl,
Stretching stargrass-straight in
Unbroken pattern.

Tilled spring fields are severed only by roads,
Tree lines, long lanes reaching, leading to farm houses
Huddled tightly like frightened ones
hugging barns, silos, elms
fixed in these windy Midwestern fields.

Cell towers climb skyward above outstretched steeples
Of history. This highway, I-80 erupts in a crest
Crumpling up from the earth in

The dull rumbling growl
Of wheels rolling.

Twenty years ago in high air in the night sky
From Boeing heights, Cleveland—
Seen below—luminescent speckles like shining stones
Tipped, huddled in gloom against smooth shore
Far below beside Lake Erie.

KITE

One
can feel
that fluttering
tug, rising skyward, tied in flight—
that touch like fish on a line in the fishpond.
Kite flyer eyes gaze skyward at a pliable diamond dancing
from side to side five miles high. This aspirant action—
this aspiration to control, curb, constrain,
command this soaring diamond
held between heaven and
earth, heard in
submissive
resistance
in currents
of winds,
or resistant
submission
to hands
that
hold
far
far
be—
low.

www.ingramcontent.com/pod-product-compliance
Lightning Source LLC
Chambersburg PA
CBHW030532080526
44586CB00011B/403